Our Skin is Special

By Vikki McIntyre

Illustrated by Luna Undra

We respect and honour Aboriginal and Torres Strait Islander Elders past, present and future. We acknowledge the stories, traditions and living cultures of Aboriginal and Torres Strait Islander peoples on this land and commit to building a brighter future together.

Library For All Ltd.

Our skin is special

Our skin is special. It does so many things, like regulating our body temperature and letting us know when we touch something too hot or too cold.

Our skin protects our bodies, keeps us healthy, and shows who we are.

But sometimes, skin can get sick. Common skin problems for our mob include scabies, impetigo, fungal infections, and insect bites.

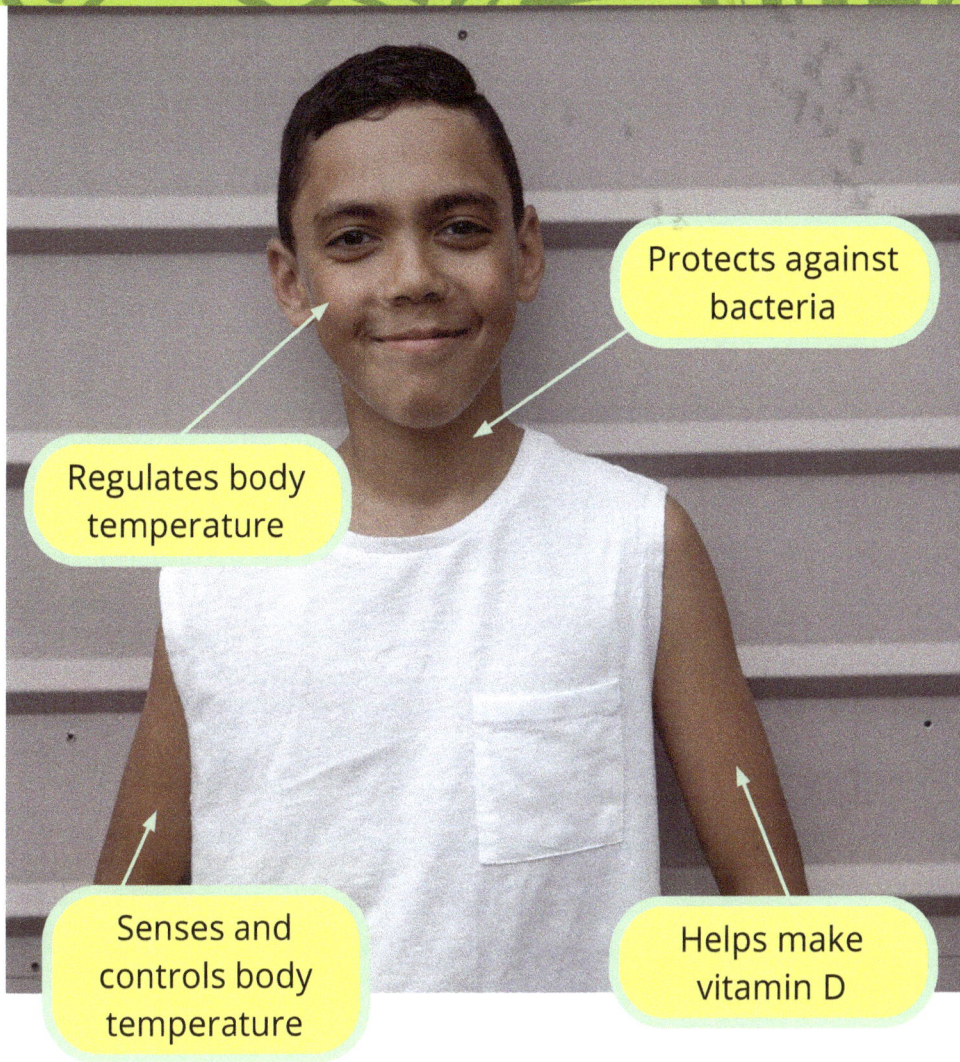

Protects against bacteria

Regulates body temperature

Senses and controls body temperature

Helps make vitamin D

Let's learn about these diseases, how to look after our skin, and how traditional bush medicines and western medicines can help.

What are scabies and impetigo?

Scabies is a skin disease caused by tiny mites that burrow under your skin. It makes your skin itchy, especially at night, and can cause sores from scratching. You might see tiny bumps or lines where the mites have burrowed.

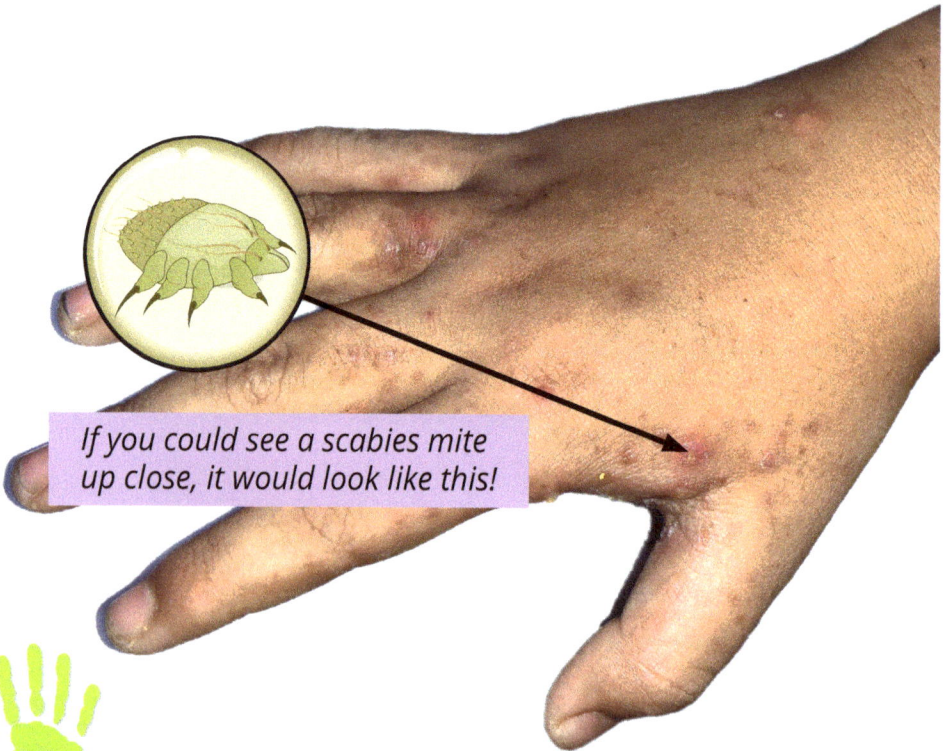

If you could see a scabies mite up close, it would look like this!

Impetigo (or school sores) happens when germs get into the cuts or scratches on your skin. It makes sores that become crusty, itchy, and painful. It spreads quickly if you don't treat it.

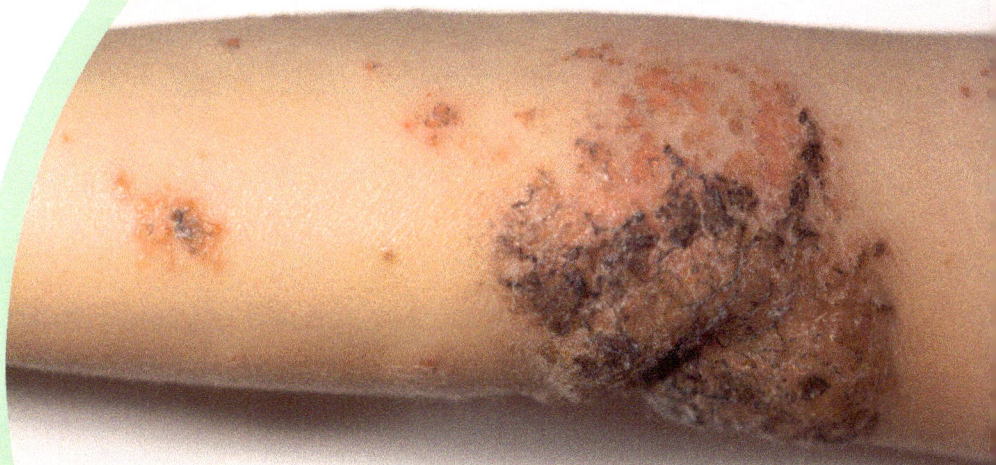

What about fungal infections and insect bites?

Fungal infections, like ringworm or athlete's foot, happen when fungus grows on your skin. They cause itchy ring-shaped red patches or flaky skin that can spread if not treated properly.

Insect bites from mozzies, ants, or sandflies can cause itchy swollen bumps. Scratching can lead to infections if the skin is broken.

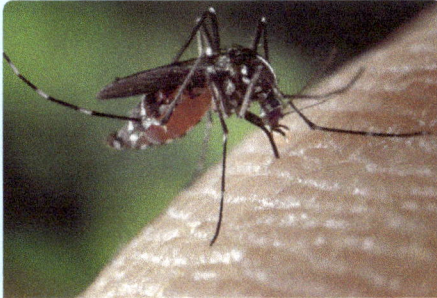

Mosquito bites can be very itchy, but try not to scratch them.

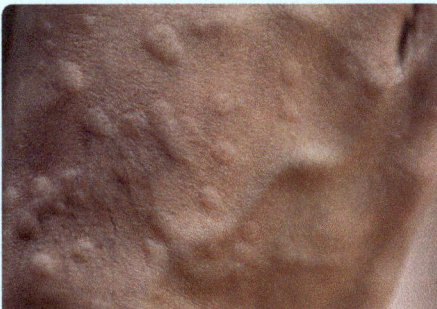

These bumps were caused by ant bites.

Caring for your skin with bush medicine

For thousands of years, mob have used bush medicines from plants to keep skin healthy. Here are some common bush medicines and their uses.

Tea tree (Melaleuca): Found near waterways, tea tree leaves can be crushed to release an oil that is good for treating skin infections, sores, insect bites, and fungal infections. It fights bacteria and fungus and helps skin heal faster.

Emu bush (Eremophila): Leaves from the emu bush help reduce swelling and fight infection. They can be boiled into washes to clean and soothe sores, skin irritations, and insect bites.

Kakadu plum (Terminalia ferdinandiana): Also known as Billy Goat plum, it is rich in vitamin C. Kakadu plum helps your skin heal and stay strong. It can be crushed and applied to sores or eaten to boost skin health from the inside out.

Western medicines for skin diseases

Doctors and clinics can give us medicines that are effective for treating skin diseases. The following table describes common skin problems and how western medicines can help.

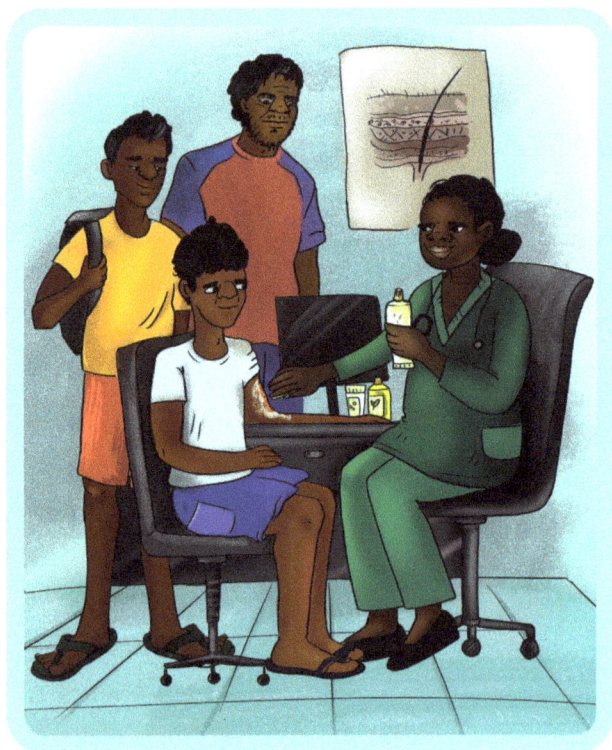

Skin problem	Western medicine	How it works
Scabies	Permethrin cream	Kills mites and eggs
	Ivermectin tablets	Treats mites from inside your body
Impetigo	Antibiotic creams (like Mupirocin)	Fights bacteria directly on sores
	Antibiotic tablets	Treats serious infections from inside your body
Fungal infections	Antifungal creams (like Clotrimazole)	Stops fungus growth on skin
	Antifungal tablets (for severe cases)	Treats fungus from inside your body
Insect bites	Antihistamine creams or tablets	Reduces itching and swelling

How bush and western medicines work together

Using bush medicines with western medicines can help your skin heal faster and stop diseases from returning. Here's how they help each other.

Skin problem	Western medicine	Bush medicine complement	Why together?
Scabies	Permethrin cream	Tea tree oil	Tea tree oil reduces itching and helps sores heal faster.
	Ivermectin tablets	Emu bush wash	Emu bush soothes the skin and fights secondary infections caused by scratching.
Impetigo	Antibiotic creams	Kakadu plum (topical)	Kakadu plum helps skin heal faster and reduces inflammation.
	Antibiotic tablets	Kakadu plum (oral)	Kakadu plum supports immune health and helps skin heal from the inside.
Fungal infections	Antifungal creams	Tea tree oil	Tea tree oil fights fungus and helps prevent the infection from spreading.
Insect bites	Antihistamine creams or tablets	Emu bush wash, tea tree oil	These bush medicines soothe itching, reduce swelling, and prevent infection caused by scratching.

Preventing skin diseases

Staying clean and looking after your skin can stop you from getting many skin diseases. Here are some things you can do to help.

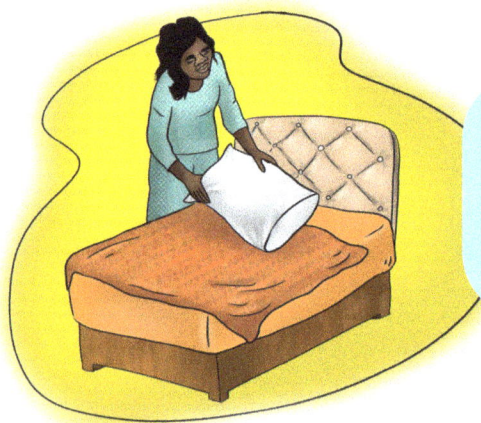

Use clean towels, sheets, blankets and pillows, and don't share them.

Wash regularly with soap, especially your hands and body.

Keep cuts and scratches clean.

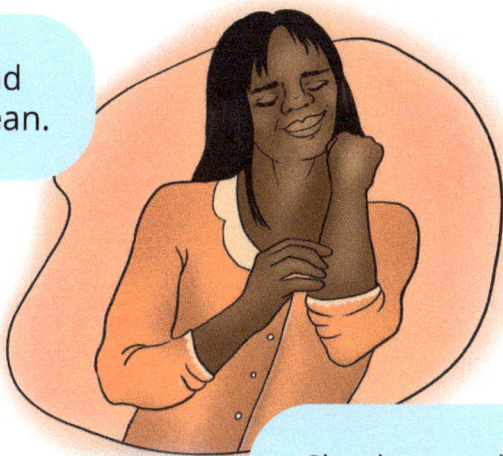

Check your skin for changes or signs of disease.

Use bush medicines to keep your skin strong and healthy.

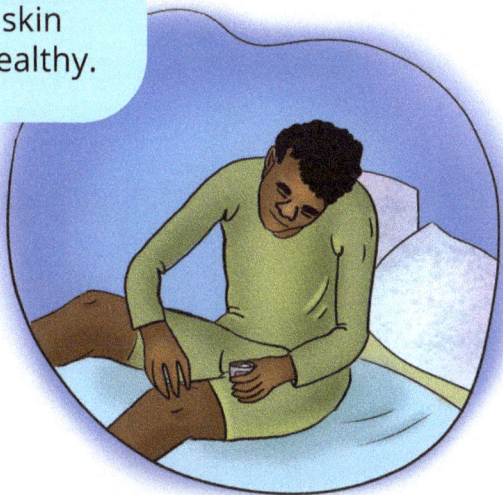

15

Covering your wounds

If you have a cut, rash, or fungal infection, it is also important to make sure you don't spread it to other people. If you scratch your skin, always wash your hands.

Some cuts require fresh air to help with healing, but sometimes it can be helpful to cover your cuts or rashes. Check with your doctor or an Elder!

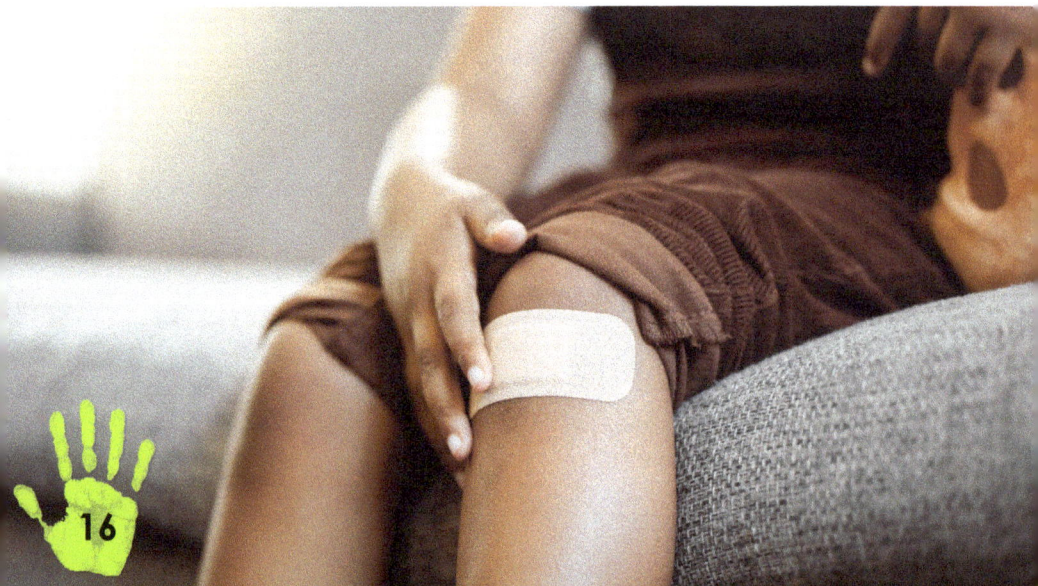

Traditionally, some people used paperbark to cover and heal wounds.

Your skin is important

Your skin is important. Using both traditional bush medicines and western medicines together keeps your skin strong, healthy, and free from disease.

This is how our mob care for each other and stay healthy and connected to culture.

Photo Credits

Page	Attribution
Page 3	Amelia Soegijono/austockphoto.com.au
Page 4	Zay Nyi Nyi/istockphoto.com
Page 4 (mite)	ttsz/istockphoto.com
Page 5	Matthew Roberge/istockphoto.com
Page 7 (top)	FotoshopTofs/pixabay.com
Page 7 (bottom)	Sinhyu Photographer/shutterstock.com
Page 8	narvikk/istockphoto.com
Page 9 (top)	Jose Maria Barres Manuel/alamy.com
Page 9 (bottom)	Leanne Atherton/austockphoto.com.au
Page 16	PeopleImages/istockphoto.com
Page 17	Lara Cain Gray

You can use these questions to talk about this book with your family, friends and teachers.

What did you learn from this book?

Describe this book in one word. Funny? Scary? Colourful? Interesting?

How did this book make you feel when you finished reading it?

What was your favourite part of this book?

Download the Library For All Reader app from libraryforall.org

About the author

Vikki McIntyre was born in Sydney and grew up in the western suburbs. Her ancestral Country is the south coast of New South Wales. She descends from the saltwater people of the Dharawal language group. Vikki is happiest when she can feel sand under her feet and smell saltwater in the air.

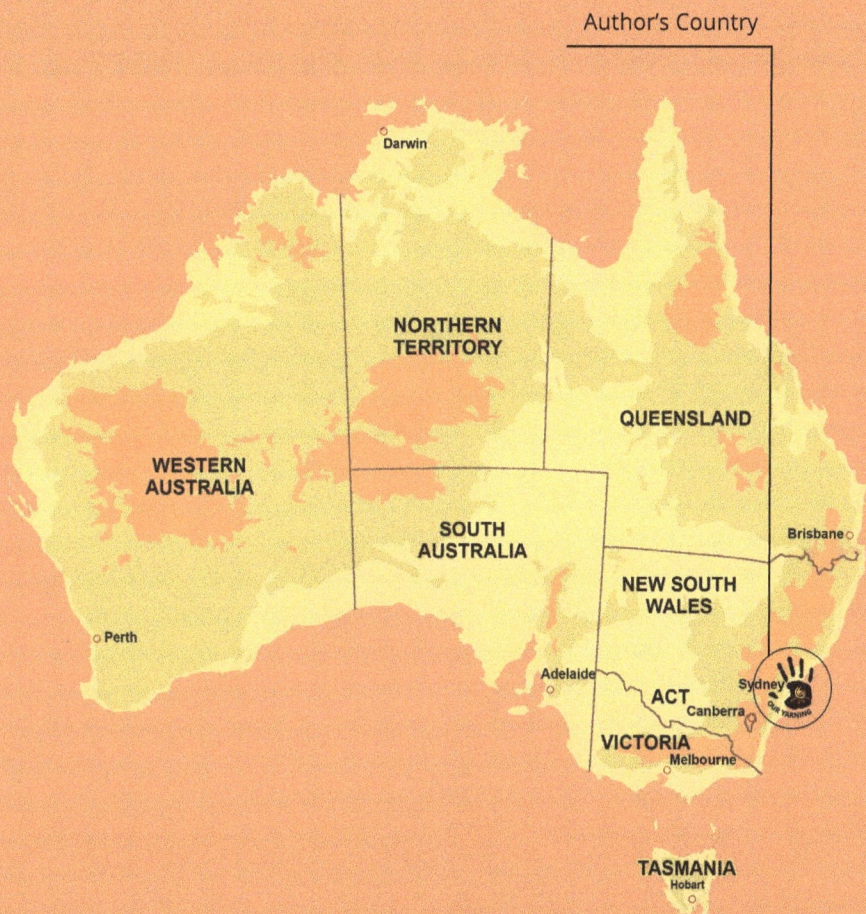

Author's Country

Darwin

NORTHERN
TERRITORY

QUEENSLAND

WESTERN
AUSTRALIA

SOUTH
AUSTRALIA

Brisbane

NEW SOUTH
WALES

Perth

Adelaide

Sydney

ACT
Canberra

VICTORIA
Melbourne

TASMANIA
Hobart

Our Yarning

The Our Yarning collection aligns with the Australian Curriculum through the Cross-Curriculum Priorities — Aboriginal and Torres Strait Islander Histories and Cultures. The collection provides an authentic opportunity for learning and embedding Aboriginal and Torres Strait Islander perspectives because it is written by Aboriginal and Torres Strait Islander people.

We know that children learn better, and enjoy reading more, when they see themselves in the stories, characters and illustrations of the books they read.

To download the app, visit the Google Play Store or Apple Store and search 'Our Yarning'.

libraryforall.org

You're reading Upper Primary

Learner – Beginner readers

Start your reading journey with short words,
big ideas and plenty of pictures.

Level 1 – Rising readers

Raise your reading level with more words,
simple sentences and exciting images.

Level 2 – Eager readers

Enjoy your reading time with familiar words,
but complex sentences.

Level 3 – Progressing readers

Develop your reading skills with creative stories
and some challenging vocabulary.

Level 4 – Fluent readers

Step up your reading skills with playful narratives,
new words and fun facts.

Middle Primary – Curious readers

Discover your world through science and stories.

Upper Primary – Adventurous readers

Explore your world through science and stories.

Library For All is an Australian not for profit organisation with a mission to make knowledge accessible to all via an innovative digital library solution. Visit us at libraryforall.org

Our Skin is Special

First published 2025

Published by Library For All Ltd
Email: info@libraryforall.org
URL: libraryforall.org

This book was made possible by the generous contributions of GSK.

Our Yarning logo design by Jason Lee, Bidjipidji Art

Original illustrations by Luna Undra

Our Skin is Special
McIntyre, Vikki
ISBN: 978-1-923594-13-5
SKU04967